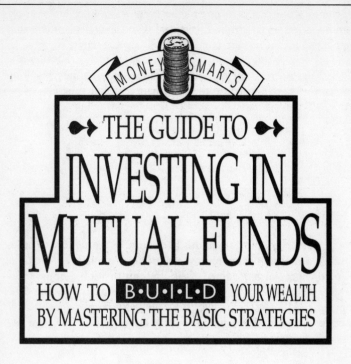

MONEY SMARTS

➤➤ THE GUIDE TO ➤➤

INVESTING IN
MUTUAL FUNDS

HOW TO B·U·I·L·D YOUR WEALTH
BY MASTERING THE BASIC STRATEGIES

by David L. Scott

The
Globe
Pequot
Press

OLD SAYBROOK, CONNECTICUT

Library of Congress Cataloging-in-Publication Data

Scott, David Logan, 1942-
     The guide to investing in mutual funds / by David L. Scott. -- 1st
ed.
          p.   cm. -- (Money smarts)
     Includes index.
     ISBN 1-56440-247-9
     1. Mutual funds.   I. Title.   II. Series.
HG4530.S39   1993
332.63'27--dc20   93-10818
                                                                CIP

Figure on page 139 courtesy of Arthur Wiesenberger Services; figure on page 140 courtesy of Morningstar, Inc.

Manufactured in the United States of America
First Edition/First Printing